DAILY REFLECTIONS
WITH MARY

Like the Apostles in the Upper Room, we can daily join ourselves in prayer with Mary our Mother.

DAILY REFLECTIONS WITH MARY

Thirty-One Prayerful Marian Reflections
And Many Popular Marian Prayers

Edited
by
REV. RAWLEY MYERS

Illustrated

CATHOLIC BOOK PUBLISHING CO.
New York

NIHIL OBSTAT: Daniel V. Flynn, J.C.D.
Censor Librorum

IMPRIMATUR: Patrick J. Sheridan
Vicar General, Archdiocese of New York

"May the Blessed Virgin ever be your light, your hope, and direct your thoughts to that homeland of heaven which is our goal and joy."

—*Pope John Paul II*

(T-220)

CONTENTS

Reflections

Prayers to Mary

Mary prays for us before God's throne.

1st Day

Our Intercessor with God

MARY prays that Jesus will change our weak hearts and make them strong and loving, just as at Cana He changed the water into wine. Our hearts so often are as weak as water and they must be changed into the wine of unselfish love. But we cannot do this alone.

Mary knows this best of all, and so she begs her Son to assist us. This is her prayer, for she knows that Jesus can make our hearts brave, as He did the cowardly hearts of the Apostles through sending the Holy Spirit on Pentecost.

Comfortable Christians, of course, do not want to change. They have been lulled into complacency. They spend too much time in their overstuffed chairs watching TV. Mary's prayers are our hope.

She will help us be true Christ-followers, people who, like Christ, aid others. A Christian unwilling to make sacrifices for others is not really a Christian at all. A Christian is to imitate Christ. Christ gave His life for others.

There are all around us timid, fearful, cold souls, afraid to love. Jesus taught us how to love. We must teach others. Like Jesus we must have open hearts. Like our dear Blessed Mother, we must show love in our lives. That is the best way to teach, by example.

Prayer

DEAREST Mary, loving Mother of God, help of Christians, Gate of Heaven, assist us. You are the most blessed of all creatures and the most loved by Jesus. You are our Mother also and we your children are devoted to you.

Mother, as Jesus loved you, help us to love you. We are most grateful that Jesus generously gave you to us to be our Mother, our helper, our protector. Please take care of us and our families and our loved ones and all who are in need. Amen.

Mary's humility drew God to her.

2nd Day

Model of Humility

HUMILITY is the beginning of wisdom. Our dear Blessed Mother gave us a beautiful example of humility, and so she is the Seat of Wisdom. She shows us that the humble can do great things. Humility is a virtue not of our nothingness but of God's greatness.

All the great things pride cannot do, humility can do easily. The will that loses its pride gains its strength. Humble souls know that God has chosen them because they are little. Humility keeps the head clear, and nothing is so necessary in the spiritual life as keeping the head clear.

With humble hearts, like Mary, we can help others. Like Jesus we can "go about doing good." And in so doing we are imparting the art of love. This lesson of ours is taken to heart by others because we are not pompous and haughty. Jesus said His followers must be servants. He Himself gave us the beautiful example of washing the feet of the Apostles at the Last Supper. Mary too taught love so well because always in helping others she was so humble and gracious.

What the world needs most these days is love. Not just to sing about it or talk about it, but for Christ-followers to show His love. We need people like Mary willing to give but expecting nothing in return. They do not ask, "What's in it for me?" They are giving individuals. Such people are indeed true Christians.

Prayer

D EAR Blessed Mother, you show me that when I do God's will I am praising Him best of all. Glory to His Holy Name. You, O Mother, are the greatest of the saints, and you are my wonderful Mother in heaven. Your greatest desire is to help us, your children.

I pray to you, I praise you, I love you, dear Mother. The words of the Bible apply to you, "You are all fair, O my love; and there is no spot in you. . . . Who is this who comes like the dawn, fair as the moon, bright as the sun?" Amen.

In her generosity Mary appeared to St. Bernadette.

3rd Day

Exemplar of Generosity

OUR heavenly Mother shows us that real love is not self-centered. In fact, selfish love is not love at all. Love is something we give away. True love is thinking of others and helping them. Such love is difficult for us because we have grown up in a pleasure-loving society. TV has brainwashed us into thinking that comfort, pleasure, and entertainment are the goals of life. How different was Jesus. How different was His holy Mother.

Mary prays daily that we, her children, will be more generous, like her Son. Her hope is that all her children will be like Jesus.

Many today have countless possessions, but they are not happy. You cannot buy happiness. It's not for sale. You can own everything in the world and still be unhappy. Indeed some of the most wretched people are the richest. For possessions are external, and happiness is in the heart. We gain happiness by giving it away. As St. Francis of Assisi said, "it is in giving that we receive."

Though many are comfortable and have much more than their parents, Bishop Sheen has said, "There never was a time in the history of the world when more people were more unhappy than they are today." Mary, generous, gracious, giving, reaching out to help her neighbors in need in Nazareth, shows us the way to be happy.

Prayer

L OVING Mother, I bless you. With the angel Gabriel I say, "Blessed are you among women." You are fairest of all creatures, the most beautiful individual to ever come from the hand of God. Thank you, Mother, for your generosity in bringing Jesus into the world amid many trials; thank you for helping me so much; thank you for looking after me and my beloved ones.

Thank you, Mary, for standing beside Jesus when everyone else had run away. Thank you, thank you for so many things, my Blessed Mother. Amen.

From the stump of Jesse a bud will blossom

Mary shows Christ to human beings.

4th Day

Christ-Bearer

PEOPLE are looking for Christ in Christians. They want to see Jesus. His disciples in the world now are supposed to show Christ by our kindness. Do others see Jesus in observing you? A person who claims to be a Christ-follower should act like Christ. There is no doubt that when people looked at the Blessed Mother they thought of Jesus.

What Christianity needs today is not bigger churches but better Christians in them. Jesus is not interested in fine buildings; He is interested in kinder individuals. It is not fancy buildings that make a good parish, it is love in the hearts of the parishioners.

Mary prays daily that the love of Jesus will be stirred up in our hearts. Christ promised to be with His followers until the end of time.

But He cannot be seen by others unless Christians show His love.

When we are petty, humorless, angry, are we true to Christ? How can those outside the Church believe that we are disciples of the gentle Jesus? When Christians are gloomy and pessimistic, unbelievers remark, "They say that Christ is with them, but they act no differently than we do." And Mary's heart fills with sorrow.

A Christ-follower lacking in love keeps people away from Christ. But when the faithful, like Mary, are loving, gracious, smiling, and generous, others are attracted to our Lord.

Prayer

O Mary, God adorned you with multiple gifts and graces. The angel Gabriel said you were full of grace. O gracious Mother, how loving you are and how worthy of our praise and gratitude.

We thank you for giving divine wisdom to the world. Through you the Redeemer came to us to save us. Through you the Son of God entered time and told us the message of heaven. Light dispelled our darkness because you, dear Mary, said Yes to God. We are grateful. We thank you with all our hearts. Amen.

Mary accepted God's will for her.

5th Day

Doer of God's Will

WHEN the angel came to Mary she immediately replied that whatever God wished she wished. And so "the Word was made flesh." The greatest event in all of history took place because Mary consented. She could have said No, but she said Yes.

May we become like our Mother. God wants each of us to do His will. It is in this way that we will be happy. God has a special assignment for each of us; great or small is not important. The important thing is to do as our heavenly Father desires. God wants to use you, as He used Mary, to give His love to the world. We are all called to be channels of kindness. Our vocation is to add to the love in the world.

If we pray to the Blessed Mother she will help us fulfill our vocation. Then we will be kinder to our family, our neighbors, and those in need. We will make our world, small as it is, a better place.

Jesus is our model. He came to bring the love of God to us. He established a kingdom of love on earth. We are His disciples. We are also to spread the love of God. We are to be His instruments for doing good.

The more we know and love Jesus, the more we will follow Him. Mary who knew Him better than anyone will help us know Him more. Let us pray to our Blessed Mother for this great blessing.

Prayer

THE world was plunged into darkness and despair before you said Yes to God, dear Mary. We can never begin to repay you for consenting to be the Mother of the Savior. You never thought of yourself or the difficulties involved, but only that you could help us. Thank you, dearest Mother, thank you.

O Blessed Lady, you are our example. We are timid and tearful; help us to have a little of your courage and faith. We are afraid; give us a little of your beautiful trust in God. We are in need of greater faith and hope; Mother, pray for us. Amen.

My soul magnifies the Lord and my spirit rejoices in God my Saviour

Mary went to visit and help Elizabeth.

6th Day

Helper of Others

MARY all her life reached out to help others. With a warm word, a cheerful smile, a gracious act of kindness, Mary made her neighbors feel better. May we be more like her. Do we write a little note of cheer or make a telephone call to show our concern, or go to our neighbor in need?

There are so many people around us who are lonely. We can make their whole day happier by showing a little interest in them, by visiting them, by saying a few cheerful words. Too many who call themselves Christians say, "I don't want to interfere," but what they really mean is, "I don't want to be bothered."

Mary will help us to be kinder, if we ask her. She will give us the strength to do the nice thing, to go the extra mile. It was her prayers and her beautiful example that held the Apostles together when Jesus returned to heaven. They wanted to run away, as they had run away in the Garden of Gethsemane, but Mary was there. No creature prayed the way she prayed. And they prayed with her, and the Holy Spirit came to them at Pentecost, and they became true Apostles, bold and brave.

Let us then pray to Mary for her assistance. How powerful her prayers are. Did not Jesus at the wedding feast change His mind because she asked Him to? As she gave strength to the Apostles, she will give us courage. She will help us be more like Christ in assisting others.

Prayer

WE know that we cannot really help people, but Jesus can. We ask you, Mother, to beg Him for the graces we all need and especially we pray for those who are troubled and forlorn. Ask Him to heal in soul and body both us and them.

No doubt you said to the people in Nazareth, "I cannot help you, but my Son can. I will tell my Son about you and ask Him to assist you. He will do something for you, I am sure." Please Mary, ask your Son to help us now. Thank you very much. Amen.

Mary dedicated herself to God from the time she entered the Temple as a child.

7th Day

Model of True Devotion

YOUR Mother in heaven loves you very much. She expects good things from you. Like all mothers, Mary expects you to succeed. She believes in you, and she wishes to increase your faith and hope.

Mary wishes you success, but, of course, success to her is not the same as success to the world. Success to Mary means that you will become more Christlike. Nothing else matters. Kindness is the measure of Christian success. Are you a kind person? Are you working at being kinder? Do you try to do at least one kind thing for someone every day?

Money, power, and popularity are not the signs of Christian success. Kindness is. These other things are unimportant to Mary. To her the whole purpose of life is to open your heart and let out the love Jesus has given you. She wants you to share His love with others.

First, we must give our love to God. We should be grateful to our heavenly Father for His countless daily blessings. We can show our appreciation by helping our neighbor, as God has helped us.

Our Mother wants us to make room for the love of Jesus in our hearts. We please her when we please her Son. And we please Him by reaching out to our neighbor in need. Too many spend their time in fruitless self-pity. They think of themselves too much and feel sorry for themselves. The cure for loneliness is to help others, as Jesus did.

Prayer

A CHILD often resembles its mother. We pray to you, dear Mary, that we may be more like you. You are the most loving and understanding creature of all.

Your Son emptied Himself for us, giving His life to save us. By this He freed us from the slavery of sin. You, O Mother, know how much it cost Him to die for us; you stood beneath the Cross and watched Him die. He loved us unto death. Please do not let all this sorrow and suffering be in vain. Help me, Mother. Bless me and assist me. Amen.

*Mary is the "brilliant star" to whom
our prayers rise like incense.*

8th Day

Mother of Life and Light and Beauty

WITH childlike pleading we turn to Mary,
our Mother, calling to her for help. As a
child, we want our Mother. Her mercy is great
beyond words, and we beg her assistance. We
ask her to weave a garment of love to warm
our hearts and protect us from the cold world.

We beseech her to send the angels to look
after us and our home and family. She is
God's masterpiece, the Queen of heaven and
earth, the glory of the people, brilliant star,
delight of the faithful.

St. Gertrude said of her, "Hail, white lily of
the Holy Trinity; hail, beautiful flower of God,
please feed our souls with your goodness."

We ask Mary to use her great influence to gain graces for us, for we are weak and frail like small children, but we are her children. Jesus gave us to her. St. Gertrude addressed her as "the radiant rose of heavenly fragrance, red and effulgent, Daughter of the Eternal Father, Spouse of the Holy Spirit, Virgin most glorious, most meek, sweet, compassionate and gracious."

Mary is our refuge, our delight, stream of everlasting life, never-failing spring of blessings, and consoler of the sorrowing. An old Irish litany calls her, "Sun of all maidens, full moon of beauty, Mother of generosity, melody of the harp, heart without sin." And it concludes, "O Virgin, Mother, may I go to heaven to visit you!"

Prayer

MOTHER of life and light and beauty, come to us. Mother undefiled, Virgin blessed beyond compare, sweet love, great Lady, guide of pilgrims, strength of our weakness, riches of our poverty, healer of our pain, comforter of our worries, hope of our salvation, Mother of all good things, Mother of the Redeemer and His constant companion, help us, please do help us and bless us and gain for us the graces we need, for we are your small children and we do not know the way. Thank you, Mother. Amen.

Mary watched lovingly over Jesus on earth.

9th Day

Our Most Loving Mother

WE look to Mary, Mother of orphans, for we are like little lost children in the darkness of this world. She is the ladder to heaven, as an eighth century prayer calls her. She is "our life, our sweetness, and our hope." As she said, "all generations shall call me blessed."

The Church has ever thrilled with devotion to Mary. In loving her we imitate Jesus who loved her most of all.

In the fullness of time God sent His Son, born of Mary. God chose a Mother worthy of His Son. She was the first holy tabernacle. No nobler one can be thought of. But best of all for us, she is our Mother. Our child's heart pleads for her to come to our assistance. We beg, childlike, to be aided by her prayers.

St. Stanislaus was asked how much he loved Mary and said, "She is my Mother. What else can I say?"

The glory of Our Lady is her Son. We, like Jesus, blessedly respect her as our Mother. Like a small child, we hold fast to her.

In this life we cannot expect to understand everything about God's plans. Even Mary did not. "She kept all these things, pondering them in her heart." There is no reason why we small creatures should comprehend the great master plan of the Creator. But we do know what a mother is and we know Mary is our Mother. A mother is the most loving person on earth, and Mary is the most loving mother.

Prayer

BELOVED Mother, in you the heavens exult and the earth rejoices and the angels sing praise to you and we poor pilgrims glory in the fact that we are your children. St. Anthony of Padua said, "The Name of Mary has ever been joy to the heart and honey to the month."

We ask, Mother, that by your loving intercession we may be delivered from evil here on earth and attain the eternal joy of heaven. We rejoice in you, Mary, our Mother, and we reverence you for all your goodness. Amen.

*Mary obtains the sweetness of
God's grace for us.*

10th Day

Our Protector against Evil

GOD was pleased with Mary. She was not compelled to assent to His request that she be the Mother of the Messiah. She could have said No. A spiritual writer tells us that all nature held its breath awaiting her answer. And her answer was immediate and affirmative. Although she was free to have said No to God, she could never say No to Him, so great was her love. She quickly replied that she wanted only to do God's will.

And so Mary gave birth to the Child, nursed Him, and protected Him, took care of Him, loved Him, trained Him, taught Him, and she never left Him. And, oh, how she suffered for Him. Mary was rich in grace, full of unselfish love. She, a woman of constant kindness, is Our Lady of Grace. She is God's treasure, the Mother of all human beings.

A child can forget its mother, but a mother can never forget her child. And this is even more true of our Blessed Mother. And so we petition her to protect us from evil. The devil goes about like a roaring lion, seeking to devour and destroy all, but especially those closest to Christ. But Mary who hates sin conquers evil.

She comes to our assistance, as did our own mother when we were small and cried for her. The evil one assaults us, but Mary is far more powerful than he. As St. Alphonsus said, "Protect me, Mother, and I need not fear."

Mary, like the loving mother that she is, is waiting to come to our aid, to bring us new life, sweetness and hope.

Prayer

O Lady Mary, Mother of God, have mercy on us. Deliver us from danger, O glorious Mother, and grant to us, who lovingly honor you, your help and protection. By your intercession keep us from sin and the bondage of the evil one.

Hail, Holy Mary, who brought forth the King, come to our assistance. Blessed are you, O gracious Mary, in your kindness. Mercifully grant that we who approach you and ask for good things may rejoice to obtain them. Amen.

*Mary's heart was ever united with Jesus—
even in suffering.*

11th Day

Exemplar of Union with Jesus

WE trust Mary's heart to be always near.
Like a good mother she is ever teaching us. Your mother was your first teacher
and your best teacher. So is Mary.

Our Mother Mary seeks to have her children pray and do penance, for she knows
well, in her wondrous wisdom, that this is the
way to happiness and to heaven. This has always been her message when she appeared in
the world. We must pray and sacrifice so that
we will grow closer to Christ. Prayer and penance purify the soul and empty the heart of
pride, so her Son can come in. Because she is
full of mercy and loves us so much she wishes
this for us. She wants her children to be
happy, and this is the only way to happiness.

Mary has no greater desire than to make us Christlike. Dante said she is the one "by whom the key did open to God's love."

Mary is Mother Most Amiable. She, the first tabernacle, is lovely, loving, and lovable. Jesus loves Mary most of all. He loves her not only because she was His Mother but also because she is filled with goodness and beauty of soul. He loved her as a baby, as a child, and as an adult. She was the person closest to Christ. She was always near Him, at least in spirit. Her thoughts and heart were ever with Him, even when He was far away.

Mary was the first to hold Him in her arms; He heard her soothing voice, and looked into her loving eyes. She was His all in all. He was everything to her. Through their intimate association, their hearts were as one.

Prayer

NOURISH us, possess us, govern us, help us to grow in love, dear Mary.

Mother of God, immaculate, innocent, spotless, holy, sinless, more beautiful than beauty, dwelling-place of Jesus, pure as the snow, Mother, Queen of Home and Family, bless our family, parents and children. Marriage is so sacred to God that He made it a great sacrament. Bless all marriages, Mother. You knew the joy of the Holy Family; give grace to our family. Amen.

Mary attained true greatness by her holiness.

12th Day

Model of True Greatness

MARY has many titles of great beauty. She is the sinless one, though she lived in the world in the midst of sin; she is Mother Most Pure. Her prayers are powerful. We call her Help of Christians. She intervenes and intercedes for her children. She takes us in her loving arms and carries us along, as she did the Christ Child. What an inspiration to know she is always near.

Jesus was ever a part of Mary's existence, and the all-holy Son of Mary loved her with the most beautiful love in the world. He remembered her singing Him lullabies, teaching Him His prayers, telling Him Bible stories, working, cleaning, washing, cooking, sweeping, and yet always having time for Him. And He returned her gracious love with gratitude. Should we do less?

We marvel at the goodness of our Mother. We admire her, honor her, and bless her. How magnificent she is. No wonder she has so much influence with her Son. Joyfully we congratulate her, especially for her loving humility, never taking any credit for herself.

Beautiful Lady, we cherish you deep in our hearts. Bountiful Lady, we are grateful for your generous graces.

Grace comes from her like rain, and it is as welcome to our souls as moisture to a desert flower.

Prayer

WE implore humbly the help of our Mother, dear Mary. Bless our homes. May all hearts in our homes be kind and courteous and considerate and loving.

Dear Mother. Hear our pleas and prayers.

Virgin Rose, so great in virtue, beauty and charm; O loving Mother, come. Assist us in our helplessness. Bring love to our lives; we live in a drab and often loveless world. We sing of your goodness, Blessed Mother, and we know that you will help us.

We feel your motherly arms around us, dear Mary, and we know that we are safe. The wonder of your love is with us. You will guide us home to God. Amen.

*As Queen of Heaven and Earth, Mary has
the power to help us.*

13th Day
Our Advocate

MARY is our advocate. She pleads for us.
She is the Mother of Good Counsel. She
guides us. Let us listen to our Mother. We
spend too much time watching television and
taking on the worldly philosophy which tells
us comfort and pleasure are the goals of life.
That is not what Jesus taught. That is not
what our Mother tells us.

Mothers are wise. Mary knows what is best
for you. She knows well the way to heaven,
and it is not in making money and piling up
possessions, so we have no time for her Son.
We will be wise if we listen to her, Seat of
Wisdom, and serve Jesus.

We are often at the crossroads in life. Follow Mary. We often suffer. Follow Mary, who
knew many sorrows. When we imitate her ex-

ample of quiet prayer and faith, when we live according to her motherly counsel, with humility, we live after the heart of her own Son. We like children are ignorant of spiritual things. Our Lady, prudent and knowing, tells us that the reason for our existence is to be Christlike.

Mary's whole life was a continual prayer. A good person is a prayer. Mary was always thinking of Jesus. Because she prayed, great were her graces. Because she prayed, she saw clearly. She can help us for we have many muddled ideas.

Prayer

MAY Christ our true God have mercy on us and save us by the prayers of His spotless and all-pure Mother. She is our Lady, Refuge of Sinners, and Our Lady of Grace and Our Lady of Perpetual Help. Show us, dear Mother, your blessings. Hoping in you, we will not fail. You will rescue us.

We admire your humility, Mary. Because we are poor sinners, ignorant, and we are often proud. Help us to be humble. We ask your mercy. You are the joy of the just and the door through which sinners pass to heaven to be with God, our gracious Father. There is no sinner on earth so accursed as to be deprived of your mercy, Mother. You told St. Bridget this. So we sinners ask your help. Amen.

The Lord begot me the first born of His ways

God chose Mary and filled her with grace and glory.

14th Day

Our Model and Helper

THE Blessed Mother is our beautiful model. She shows us how to live. At the Annunciation she said to God, "I will," and because of this God was once more admitted into the world among His children. We are grateful for her unselfish and gracious goodness in making it possible for Jesus to come to us.

Cardinal Newman wrote, "She is not like earthly beauty, but the morning star, bright and musical, breathing purity, infusing peace. We in the dark night, wandering in the bleak wilderness, implore God to guide us to her Son and home."

Not only is Mary our model but she is our most willing helper. Cardinal Newman said, "God gave us Mary for a support in our weakness. She is the Mother of all the living, hope for the weak, a refuge for our sinfulness, a comforter of the afflicted. We kiss the hem of her garment and kneel in the shadow of her throne. We admire her as a woman of fortitude and self-surrender. And now in heaven, she is full of grace and glory."

This is our Mother, our help and our hope, and we must turn to her frequently in prayer. We ask our beloved Mother to speak to her Son for us. St. Bernard said, "Following Mary, you will never lose your way. Praying to her, you will never sink into despair.... With her support, you will never fall.... And with her help, you will reach your heavenly goal."

Prayer

HOLY Mary, Immaculate Virgin, Mother of God, I choose you for my Mother and advocate. Let me not depart from you today, but help me to do my duty. Let me be your devoted servant: assist me in all my actions, and forsake me not at the hour of my death. O Mary, conceived without sin, pray for us who have recourse to you.

I fly to your patronage, O holy Mother of God; despise not my petitions but deliver me from danger, O glorious and blessed Virgin. Pray for us, O holy Mother of God, that we may be made worthy of the promises of Christ. Amen.

*Mary showed the Angel Gabriel the same
hospitality she showed all others.*

15th Day

Angel of Mercy

WHEN people came to Mary at Nazareth
she always helped them. We cannot
conceive of anyone knocking on her door and
asking for aid leaving empty-handed. If she
was this gracious when she was on earth,
now that she is in heaven, the Queen of
Heaven, closer still to Christ, she is even more
gracious.

Not only did Mary not turn anyone away,
she invited in wayfarers. She asked them to
sit down with Jesus and Joseph and herself at
their table, and they would share their food
with the travelers. And if it was cold and their
visitors had nowhere to sleep, Mary would fix
blankets for them by the fire and give them
shelter for the night.

We can think of Mary doing nothing less. If
persons were sick in the village, she was

there. She brought food and comfort and cleaned their house and helped them any way she could. Everyone in need knew this loving angel of mercy.

We, too, should turn to her for help. She is not just a friend or neighbor; she is our Mother. Children have a right to ask their mother for assistance. When we are worried and cannot see our way, let us pray to her and the clouds will lift.

She is the Seat of Mercy and she pities us in our trials. She is especially concerned with those who are sick of soul, captives of sin. In our feeble way we look to our Mother and know that she will never fail us.

Prayer

HOLY Virgin Mary, Mother of Jesus and my Mother, keep me from sin. Protect me in all dangers of soul and body. Help me today in my work; help me to be faithful to you so that I may glorify God and save my soul.

Holy Mother Mary, I place myself under your powerful protection and ask the help of your intercession. Immaculate Virgin, beautiful Mother, Morning Star, light the way for me so that I may follow the path of Jesus. May I this day be cheerful, pleasant, and kind in my dealings with others. Amen.

Mary can give us the sweet grace of a happy death.

16th Day

Our Intercessor at Death

CARDINAL Newman wrote, "Place me under Mary's smile. It will be blessed indeed to have her at your side at the hour of death, as we pray so often in the Hail Mary, for she is more tender than any earthly mother. If she is there all will be well, and if we strive to be faithful, she will be there. And she will take you home with her to see her Son in heaven where there is perfect peace and serene joy and love unutterable."

Mary is full of grace. Sin had no part in her. She showed so beautifully what God can do with human nature if a person lets Him. Mary reversed the Fall, and yet she would be the first to say that her glories were for the sake of Jesus, given her by God.

Mary is "our tainted nature's solitary boast," as the English poet Wordsworth said.

She from the first was clothed in sanctity. She is grace and smiling light. God meant in the beginning to walk with human beings in the world, but humanity in pride rejected Him. He then had to choose another way. And so He came to a young maiden in Nazareth and asked her to admit Him again into His world. Her answer was an immediate Yes.

We ask our Blessed Mother to exert over our hearts a gentle sway, so that we may be ever faithful to Jesus, her Son. Archbishop Fulton J. Sheen wrote, "It is a constant tradition of the Catholic Church that anyone truly devoted to Mary is never lost."

Prayer

WE ask you, Mary, with Jesus and Joseph, to give us a happy death. Assist us in our last agony. May we breathe forth our soul in peace with you. We offer you our heart and soul; may we one day be with you in heaven.

We ask you, Mary, with Jesus and Joseph, to give those who have died eternal rest. Let perpetual light shine upon them. May they know the glory and love and light and joy of heaven.

Holy Mother, I place myself under your blue mantle of love. Look with kindness upon me, a poor sinner, your little, loving child. Amen.

Hearken, O daughter, the Lord, thy God, shall greatly desire thy beauty

Mary's beauty of soul pleased God.

17th Day

Model of Resignation to God's Will

FOR thirty years Mary saw and heard Jesus and conversed with Him daily. He was the light of her life, her joy, her inspiration, her everything. He gave not a look but that she understood it better than if He had expressed a thousand words. And to pray with Him each day was like paradise: it made her heart soar and her soul feel on fire.

Mary had taught Him His prayers in the beginning, but He soon, even as a Boy, overtook her in devotion and intensity. To look at His face when He was at prayer was to see that He was out of this world, lost in God.

Finally, however, there came the time when He would deny Himself His dear Mother's love and affection. He must serve the Father.

He had to leave her and go out and preach to the people. It was such a sadness for Mary but she accepted it with courage. Though there was nothing she wanted more than to be with Him, she knew He must leave her.

The dread day of departure came. They needed no words to say good-bye. They looked at one another and each understood perfectly. She smiled, and in silence He left her, turning His back on His days of greatest happiness. She watched Him until He disappeared. Returning to the empty house she knelt and prayed. Her heart broke in two, but as always she offered her suffering to God.

Prayer

M OST holy and Immaculate Virgin Mary, our tender Mother, help of Christians, we dedicate ourselves to your most sweet love and holy service. We consecrate our minds and hearts to your Son, Jesus. Continue to show us your mercy. Enlighten and strengthen us. Preserve us in our faith. Make us always loyal to Jesus.

Increase the number of those who love your Son. Promote vocations. Look with compassion on the young and direct them in the ways of Jesus. And look with love on all poor sinners and on all those who are dying today. Be for all, our sweet hope, O Mary. Amen.

*Mary joined herself to the sufferings Jesus endured
for our salvation.*

18th Day

Cause of Our Joy

MARY is merciful, and so we pray, "Open to us the door of mercy, dear Mother." Hoping in her we will not be confounded. Through Mary we will be delivered from our adversaries. She is the hope of Christians. She is the font of mercy. She is full of compassion. We ask her to look down upon us poor sinners, and heal us.

Mary is especially blessed because she was always faithful. She is the shining example of loyalty to Jesus. We pray to her, standing beneath the Cross, loyal and true to the end. We ask that we may follow her example and that she will be with us "now and at the hour of our death."

Mary, Seat of Wisdom, teaches us the way to heaven. A mother is the natural teacher of the child. Let us have recourse to our Mother and learn her wise ways.

Mary is the Cause of Our Joy. She gives us happiness. She made it possible for us to be redeemed. Without her humble, gracious consent we could not have been saved from sin and our selfishness. This indeed is glad tidings. What gladness shone in Mary's eyes when she held her little Son in her arms. She gives away that joy to those who pray to her. She smiles upon us.

Prayer

MOTHER in heaven look down upon us poor sinners. We are not worthy of your love, but we are your children and we need very much. You beheld Jesus dying for sinners and know what a terrible price He paid to save us, so much does He love us; we know that you too yearn exceedingly to save your children.

Dear Mother, make our hearts burn with love for Jesus.

O Jesus, my only hope, my Savior and my God, at my last hour send to me your tender Mother, that soft-shining Star of the Sea, that she may stand by me as my sure defense. Her face, fair as the bright dawn of morning, will make me know that You love me. Amen.

His name was called JESUS

While Mary was at prayer, the Angel told her she was to be the Mother of Jesus.

19th Day

Exemplar of Prayer

SO often we feel hopelessly inadequate in life. But Mary united in heart with Jesus wishes to save us. We ask for her prayers that she will intervene with her Son, our Savior. St. Bernard of Clairvaux said, "If you fear the Father, go to the Son; if you fear the Son, go to the Mother."

Monsignor Ronald Knox wrote, "Mary is so good at sympathizing with us. We need her tender smile and the touch of her gentle hand. Mary protects us and looks after us just as she did the Christ Child. She wants to be our companion just as she was the constant companion of Jesus."

Like a good mother, Mary teaches us the way to pray. Not only did she pray often, but

44

she prayed with great confidence. Let us ask Mary to help us be sorry for our sins and make our cold, detached, earthbound hearts more considerate of others. Let us ask her to bring cleansing and healing and comfort to our minds and hearts that are now many times murky and miserable and petty.

We pray to Our Lady so that upon us her love may rest and that we be given the grace of Christ, our Lord, and an ever deeper faith.

We wish Mary, the Mother of Sorrows, to help us in our sorrows. She suffered so much and she knows how we feel.

Prayer

O most gracious Queen, as I begin another day, I dedicate myself and all I do to you. I know that you will help me. Ask your Son to bless me. Whatever pleases Him, pleases you. Your whole life is dedicated to Him. You desire nothing more than that Jesus be better known in this sinful world.

Please aid me and protect me so that I may do this, so that by my example and word others will see the kindness of a Christian. I put my trust in you, Mother, and in your Son, our sweet Savior. I hope always to be your humble servant; this is my greatest boast. Amen.

Mary told St. Bernadette, "I am the Immaculate Conception."

20th Day

Model of Holiness

MARY was an especially beautiful person, because the great beauty of her soul shone in her eyes and face. This lovely, sinless daughter of God was selfless, a lovely flower, the most glorious of all in God's garden of saints. Jesus dearly loved his Mother; as the angel said, she was overflowing with grace, holy and good.

Her days on earth were full of duties to her Son, to Joseph, to her neighbors, to the needy near and far. And when she was left alone in the world after Jesus returned to the Father, her duty was to encourage the Apostles and pray for the frail infant Church. We cannot think of her without helping someone. She is indeed the Mother of the Church, for it never would have succeeded without her.

She suffered, with her Son, the betrayal of Judas, the denial of Peter, the cowardice of the Apostles when in the Garden He was arrested and needed them the most. She saw Him covered with blood on the terrible journey up to the hill of execution. She with broken heart felt every blow as they drove the horrid spikes through His hands and feet. Tears flowed down her cheeks as He hung upon the Cross. Grief filled her as she saw Him die. O loving, good Blessed Mother, pray for us.

Prayer

O Mother of God, Mary most holy, in your kind mercy bless me and help me overcome the hardness of my heart and my indifference and complacency. You have helped me so often, so often preserved me from sin; I am most grateful.

O my Queen, do not let your graces given graciously to me go in vain. With all my heart I beg strength for my poor soul. Grant me your blessings. I need so many. And bless my loved ones. Amen.

From the stump of Jesse a bud will blossom

By giving birth to the Son of God, Mary brought heaven to earth.

21st Day

Gate of Heaven

MOST of all, dear Mary, you are the Gate of Heaven. We pray to enter the beautiful portals of paradise with your help. We are weary pilgrims on the way. When as children we came home from school it was always a joy to open the door because we knew our mother was waiting to welcome us. So we feel after our wanderings here on earth, after our exile, our Mother Mary will be waiting, for she is the Gate of Heaven. She will welcome us to our true home and happiness forever.

The very thought of light reminds us of Mary. She brought to us the blessed one who is the Light of the world. She is the Mother of Eternal Light. She is the Morning Star. "O poor, lost sinner, despair not, raise up your eyes and cast them on this beautiful star and breathe again with confidence, for she will guide you. The night is over, the day is dawning," said St. Bonaventure.

Mary is our safe harbor after the stormy sea. "Deep night hath come down on us, Mother, deep night, and we need more than ever the guide of thy light; for the darker the night, the brighter the light should be, thy beautiful, shining, O sweet Star of the Sea," wrote Father Faber.

In dangers and anguish, in doubt and temptation, she will sustain us. We have nothing to fear. "Follow her and you cannot wander, pray to her and you will have hope, as long as you look to her, you will be safe," an ancient prayer tells us.

Prayer

MOST holy Mary, my Lady, to your faithful care and special keeping I give myself. Keep me in your mercy always, and in particular be with me at the hour of my death. I commend my soul to you; you are my hope and comfort. In all my trials I look to you.

Through your intercession and by the merits of your prayers I know that one day I will see your Son and you, dear Mother, in the glorious heavenly kingdom of God. Amen.

Mary continually offers prayers for the sick and the dying.

22nd Day

Health of the Sick

S T. Gertrude said, "Let Mary be on your lips and in your heart and in your prayers. Lose not sight of her. Mary, draw near to my heart in all your splendor."

St. Bernard said, "O you who feel yourself tossed by the tempest, turn not away your eyes from the Star of the Sea, if you would avoid shipwreck. If the winds of temptation blow, if the ways of tribulation rise high, look at the star, sigh toward Mary. She will rescue you. If anger, avarice, and love of pleasure rock your small boat, seek Mary. Her eyes are upon you. If sin and troubles and worries and dread of God's judgment begin to plunge you into the gulf of sadness and despair, attach your heart to Mary."

Mary is Health of the Sick. She was an angel of mercy assisting the sick and dying. She nursed them and prayed with them. Her kindness was everywhere for everyone. She has a special love for those who have a particular devotion to her. An Irish saying states, "There is no hound in fleetness nor in chase, north wind or rapid river as quick as the Mother of Christ to the bed of death."

Our Mother will be with us in sickness and suffering, in pain and sorrow; our Mother will especially be with us at our last hour.

Prayer

O Refuge of Sinners, you have a special love for lost sheep. Help all sinners. Please plead for us. Let your Mother's love reach out to us. St. Bonaventure said that you embrace with motherly love all sinners, and you do not cease to embrace them until they look to your Son.

Mother, you are the place where we may run and be safe, in our Mother's arms. Pray constantly for the conversion of all sinners. This is your special work. You do not want one sinner to be lost. Stand guard over all your children. A holy man wrote that you say of each of us, "My Son bought your soul at a great price. Pray to Him. He will help you." Amen.

Filled with grace, Mary is able to comfort all who are afflicted.

23rd Day

Comforter of the Afflicted

MARY is the Comforter of the Afflicted. She greatly suffered in her life; she understands our sufferings and sorrows. She knew great agony of heart, more than we will ever endure.

She knows how to comfort us. There is room in her heart for all of us, even those who feel the most forsaken. We are not abandoned ever by our Mother. She is the hope of the worst sinner. She is Our Lady of Pity, ever pursuing us with great love.

The angel said to Mary, "The Lord is with you." Clothed in sanctity, she is closest to Christ, the nurse of His helpless infancy, the teacher of His youth. Her whole life was dedicated to Him; her whole life was one of untiring mindfulness of others. Her greatness was in always doing God's will. She lived to make Jesus better loved. Should we be indifferent to this?

Mary accepted all the joys and sorrows that came to her in life. She said that all things were from the hand of God. A spiritual writer wrote, "God gave us Mary for support in our weakness and consolation in our sufferings, a help in our dangers and a refuge in our sinfulness." She is, in a word, a mother, our Mother.

Mary suffered without complaint. She obeyed without murmur. She accepted sorrow without bitterness. She bowed to God's will with faith. She was a most patient person, enduring the difficulties of life because her prayers gave her courage.

Prayer

HOLIEST of Virgins, I honor you with all my heart, I praise you with all my mind, I thank you with all my soul. Mother and Queen, bless me and guard me. Keep me in your holy arms.

You are my hope. Please bless our country. Break down the walls of hatred and prejudice. Let the world live in peace. Mother of God, we sing your praises, inspire us to love your Son ever more. Amen.

Mary said to the Angel, "I am the servant of the Lord."

24th Day

Model of Service to God

MARY was highly honored because she was humble. "Behold the handmaid of the Lord," she said. God constantly makes use of the humble. The humble individual is a living sermon for all to see. What inspiration Mary gave to everyone who saw her.

Mary was the first Christ-bearer. The Savior rested beneath her heart. She cheerfully left all to take the long journey to help Elizabeth in her hour of need. Love urged her on. She rejoiced to be able to assist her cousin.

Elizabeth greeted Mary as the Blessed Mother of our Savior, and Mary gave all praise to God.

Mary prayed ceaselessly. In solitude, holy and calm she prayed. Silence is the home of rich spiritual thoughts. A person who prays is a wonderful instrument in the hands of our heavenly Father.

As Mary knelt at the crib her soul was full of joy. Though the night was cold, her heart was wrapped in warmth. In Bethlehem the people slept in darkness, but in Mary's beautiful soul there was brightness and light. Her heart sang like a melodious harp a canticle of joy. Her soul trembled as she saw the dear smile of her Son. Soon the shepherds came and with childlike faith honored the Babe. Joy upon joy. She felt she was in heaven.

Prayer

O Mother most loving, full of goodness, I entrust my life to you. If you will not help me, where can I turn? Deliver me from evil. Obtain for me the graces I need this day. Let your mother's care be with me, as it was with the Christ Child in the cave at Bethlehem.

All unworthy, I too am your child, because of the great generosity and goodness of your Son. Do not let me fall. May your humility inspire me to be humble so I will be wise enough to pray and gain the graces I need. May your kindness always be my example. Amen.

The Lord begot me the first born of His ways

Mary was chosen by God from all eternity.

25th Day

Chosen Daughter of the Father

MARY carried the Savior within her. She wrapped Him in swaddling clothes, fed Him at her breast, folded Him in her arms. She brought Him forth at the beginning and took care of Him and loved Him dearly, and at the end she was at His side and shared in His martyrdom. Her heart was pierced like His. How can He refuse her anything?

We live in an age that thinks it is sophisticated, so very smart—and it is headed into the swamp. People today are skeptical and cynical. They mock sanctity, consider religion a matter of taste, look on marriage as a temporary convenience.

The Blessed Mother does not fit into our society, insane with sex, drugs, pleasure, and self-centered pride. But those with common sense love her, love her values, which are the values of her Son, and admire this woman of silence who so loved God that she would do anything for Him.

Mary is known for her faithfulness, but we live in a disloyal world. She was unselfish, while so many around today think only of themselves. She was a woman of courage; we see so many who are cowardly, living pampered lives. We love the goodness of Mary, her concern for Jesus, and her concern for others. We admire her and feel greatly blessed to have her for our Blessed Mother.

Prayer

Y OU are all pure, O Mary, and there is no stain in you. Blessed be God for giving you this priceless gift. We implore you, Mother, for a greater faith, for hope to keep our eyes on heaven. We ask you for more love so that we can be more like your Son.

Heavenly Father, You chose the Blessed Mother to be the Mother of Your Son. Through her prayers grant us the grace to attain the glory of heaven.

St. Antoninus said that there is no one among the saints "whose heart is like the heart of the Blessed Mother." Blessed be Mary for her great love. Amen.

Mary's whole life was dedicated to Jesus.

26th Day

Our Sure Guide to Jesus

MARY'S Son was her life's joy and her glory. She endured untold sorrow for His sake. Jesus was everything to Mary. No one loved Him more than she did, no one loved Mary more than Jesus.

Jesus as a child turned to His Mother for help. So must we. We do not need an introduction to her—she is our Mother. You don't have to get an appointment to see your Mother. She is always there to assist you.

One of our most beautiful devotions to Mary is the Rosary. Sir Arnold Lunn wrote, "The Rosary has been the favorite devotion not only of the great saints but also of men of outstanding intellectual attainment. It is the prayer of simplicity and the prayer of meditation. It is for the humble and simple of heart;

it is for those of gifted mind who reflect on the holy mysteries."

Frank Sheed said, "If anyone's prayers have power with God, Our Lady's have; she is the Mother of all, and so most ready to come to our aid."

The Son of God was made man and was born of Mary. He was her faithful Son. We ask that we may be her faithful children. We know that if we remain loyal to her, she will always take care of us. She is Our Lady of Last Assurance. With her we are rich indeed. With her at our side we are safe.

Prayer

WHEN we honor you, dear Mary, we honor your Son even more. All praise for you, you give to Him. A saint said, "The grace that fills her is but the overflowing and superfluities of His incomprehensible sanctity." You, Mother, would be the first to tell us this. To praise Mary is to praise Jesus. No one knows that better than you, O Blessed Mother.

You, Mother, told St. Brigid that the devils fly even from sinners if we pronounce your holy Name with devotion. Help us to do this often. Amen.

Mary shared her spiritual gifts with Elizabeth by visiting her cousin.

27th Day

Rich in Spiritual Gifts

MOST Holy Queen, I dedicate myself to you. Help me to show the love of your beloved Son in my life, for there is nothing you want more.

In our Mother, Mary, we have a fountain of love. She is rich in spiritual gifts. She was filled with love. She wishes to give great graces to her children who are devoted to her.

We pray to Mary to help us at all times, but especially at the last hour when we are about to leave this world behind. We approach her with confidence. St. Antoninus said that Mary is the throne from which God dispenses many graces. We look to her then so that we may love her Son, Jesus, more dearly. We ask that we may love Him a little more the way she does.

St. Bernard said, "In danger, anguish, or doubt, think of Mary and call upon her."

Blessed Julian of Norwich said, "God, in Your goodness give me Yourself and it is enough for me. For if I ask anything less, it is not enough. Only in You do I have all." This thought Mary showed by her whole life. She was ever praising God and helping others.

As the old hymn tells us, "Had I but Mary's sinless heart to love Thee with, my dearest King, oh, with what bursts of fervent praise, Thy goodness, Jesus, would I sing."

Prayer

DEAR Mother, full of compassion and kindness, as you welcomed all who came to your little cottage at Nazareth with an open heart, do not forget me; or better, do not let me forget you, for I know that you always await me and welcome my visits. I am but a small child, fearful and weak. Help me, Mother.

You are my advocate. You wish to bless me and give me many graces, but my hands are so small and my heart is tiny. Thank you for your countless gifts already. Help me to be better, Mother. Amen.

All generations shall call me blessed

*We place all our hope in Mary because
she is wholly blessed by God.*

28th Day

Mary Our Hope

WE ask our Blessed Mother, our hope, to
make us belong wholly to Jesus. She
has a great love for souls. Saving souls is her
first concern. Bringing people to love her Son
is her delight.

In her lamp the oil of healing mercy always
flows. She stands with open arms so that all
will have recourse to her. As St. Bernard reminds us, it has never been heard of that she
abandons anyone. Indeed it is unthinkable.
She is always our merciful Mother.

All the saints loved Mary and hoped in her.
She who is the hope of the saints is our hope
also. St. Bernard said, "Let him who despairs
hope in her."

Our Mother invites all to come to her. She in all things is like her Son, Jesus, full of mercy and concern, ready ever to comfort us in our sorrow. St. Bernardine said, "She desires more to do us good and to impart graces to us than we desire to receive them." St. Augustine said, "O foolish ones of the world, where are you going to satisfy your hearts? Come to Jesus." Mary tells us the same.

Cardinal Newman wrote, "To have a virgin soul is to love nothing on earth in comparison to God. That soul is virginal which is ever looking for its Beloved, who is in heaven, and which sees Him in whatever is loving and beautiful upon earth."

Prayer

O Mary, I love you with my whole heart. Henceforth, with your blessings, I will strive to please you more. Please grant me, most of all, final perseverance. Help me and all poor sinners and the poor souls in purgatory. United to your loving heart, I praise God. Grant this through your Son, the source of every good.

We pray, "Leave me not at any time, dear Mary, but especially leave me not at the end, until you see me safe in heaven, blessing God and singing His mercies for all eternity." So I hope. So may it be. Amen.

Hearken, O daughter, the Lord, thy God, shall greatly desire thy beauty

God has filled Mary with grace and beauty of soul.

29th Day

Treasurer of Divine Grace

ST. Bernard said, "Virginity is praiseworthy, but humility is indispensable. Without humility, I am so bold as to think that even Mary's virginity would not have been pleasing to God."

Mary never refused God anything. St. Bonaventure called her the treasurer of divine grace. She wants to give these graces to us. If we have fallen, she stretches out her hand and raises us up.

Cardinal Newman said that Mary's face was angelic, one of beauty, and that her sinless soul drew others to her. People instinctively are attracted to goodness. There was a divine music in her voice and words. She charmed hearts. Her humility, her innocence, her simplicity, her modesty, her sincerity, and her unaffected interest in everyone made her most lovable.

Mary's one desire is that all souls be brought to Jesus. She, the most marvelous creature God ever made, is so very anxious to assist us, but, as the saints said, "she will not thrust herself upon us. When we seek her, she will give us a smile, a loving touch that will fill our weak and weary and sinful hearts with happiness and peace." Oh, for the touch of our Mother's hand. How it soothes us, comforts us, and takes away our fear. The miracle at the marriage feast at Cana is a striking instance of Mary's influence over the heart of her Son.

Prayer

D EAR Mother, in a vision you told a saint, "Until the world to come, I shall not cease to be the Mother of Mercy." Mother, the word merciful means having "a heart for the miserable." Your heart is full of compassion for all who suffer. Come to our assistance.

Mary, faithful and true to your Son to the end, do not desert your children who turn to you. You said, "God who is mighty has done great things to me." He has given you many graces to give to us, your children. Bless us with your blessings. Help us and grant us the graces we need. Amen.

At the foot of the Cross, Mary offered her Son and herself for the salvation of the world.

30th Day

Refuge of Sinners

AN old hymn says, "Your birth, O Virgin Mother of God, announced joy to the whole world." You are most beautiful and blessed. You are most gentle and kind, O Mother.

Blessed are those who have recourse to Mary. She can make us saints. St. Alphonsus Liguori says that those who honor her shall persevere to the end, which is the greatest blessing of all. Those who are devoted to her will enjoy everlasting life. St. Peter Damien said, "She can enrich us and dearly desires to do so." She invites all to call upon her. She especially loves sinners and those in need.

St. John Damascene said to Mary, "I have placed all my hope in you." We should say the same. He continued, "Please, obtain for me the forgiveness of my sins and perseverance until death." This is our plea.

The Blessed Mother said to St. Bridget, "However much people sin, if they return to me with a real purpose of amendment, I am instantly ready to welcome them; neither do I pay attention to the greatness of their sins, but the intention alone with which they come. I do not disdain to anoint and heal their wounds, for I am called and truly am, Mother of Mercy." How consoling are these words of our Mother. We look to her and pray to her and beg her to have pity on us.

Prayer

ACCEPT our love, dear Mother, and gain for us a greater love for Jesus. Blessed Mother, bless our home and family, our relatives and friends, living and dead. Bless those who are sick and those who are dying today. Bless all the souls in purgatory, especially those who were closest to us in this life and those who helped us the most.

Mother protect my loved ones, protect me. Keep us close to your loving, generous, gracious heart. And we will be safe. Keep us close until the day of our death; help us always to be faithful to your Son so that we can rejoice with you and Him forever in the glorious, heavenly kingdom of God. Amen.

Although her heart was pierced with sorrow,
Mary remained faithful to God's plan for her.

31st Day

Model of Faithfulness

THERE are so many beautiful titles for
Mary in her litany. We call her Mother of
Good Counsel. We pray to her for guidance.
In this life we are often like little lost children.

We address our Mother as Virgin Most
Merciful. We need so very much, not only
light to see our way, but her blessings. We ask
our dear Mother to take us by the hand.

She is Virgin Most Faithful. Mary was loyal
and true to Jesus to the end. All the brave
Apostles, with all their bragging about how
they would defend Christ, all "fled into the
night" in the garden when He was arrested,
when He needed them the most.

John, the youth, at length, felt ashamed and came back. But Mary was ever-faithful. What a wonderful example our Mother is for us. She, the first Christian, will help us to be like her, loyal and faithful to the end. That is what it means to be a Christ-follower.

Mary is called the Seat of Wisdom. How very much we need wisdom in these foolish times. So many just follow the crowd. So many Christians are unthinking and do whatever is popular. We beg our Mother for wisdom to be wise in a world where so very often common sense is lacking.

Prayer

D EAR Mother, you are the wise and loving Mother who enables us to gain eternal life and happiness in God's home for all eternity, where there will be love and goodness, joy and peace.

I pray to you for good health, for forgiveness from your Son, and for strength and consolation in our weakening on our weary way. And since you are my Mother, I know you will help me and be always there when I call. Amen.

At Cana, Mary obtained Jesus' first miracle. In heaven, she now intercedes for us with her Son.

PRAYERS TO MARY

Hail Mary

HAIL Mary, full of grace, the Lord is with thee. Blessed art thou amongst women and blessed is the fruit of thy womb, Jesus.

Holy Mary, Mother of God, pray for us sinners, now and at the hour of our death. Amen.

Hail, Holy Queen

HAIL, holy Queen, Mother of mercy: hail, our life, our sweetness, and our hope; to you do we cry, poor banished children of Eve; to you do we send up our sighs, mourning, and weeping in this valley of tears.

Turn then, most gracious advocate, your eyes of mercy toward us; and after this our exile show unto us the blessed fruit of your womb, Jesus; O clement, O loving, O sweet Virgin Mary. Amen.

Memorare

REMEMBER, O most gracious Virgin Mary, that never was it known, that anyone who fled to your protection, implored your help, or sought your intercession was left unaided. Inspired by this confidence, I fly unto you, O Virgin of virgins, my Mother.

To you I come, before you I stand, sinful and sorrow. O Mother of the Word Incarnate, despise not my petitions, but in your mercy hear and answer me. Amen.

We Fly to Your Patronage

(Sub tuum praesidium)

WE fly to your patronage, O holy Mother of God; despise not our petitions in our necessities, but deliver us always from all dangers, O glorious and blessed Virgin.

The Angel of the Lord

(Angelus Domini)

During the year (outside of Paschal Season)

℣. The Angel of the Lord declared unto Mary,

℟. *And she conceived of the Holy Spirit.*

Hail Mary. . . .

℣. Behold the handmaid of the Lord,

℟. *Be it done unto me according to your word.*

Hail Mary. . . .

℣. And the Word was made flesh,

℟. *And dwelt among us.*

Hail Mary. . . .

℣. Pray for us, O holy Mother of God,

℟. *That we may be made worthy of the promises of Christ.*

Let us pray. Pour forth, we beg You, O Lord, Your grace into our hearts: that we, to whom the Incarnation of Christ Your Son was made known by the message of an Angel, may by His Passion and Cross be brought to the glory of His Resurrection. Through the same Christ our Lord. ℟. *Amen.*

Queen of Heaven

(Regina Caeli)

During the Easter Season

Queen of Heaven, rejoice, alleluia:
For He whom you merited to bear, alleluia,
Has risen, as He said, alleluia.
Pray for us to God, alleluia.

℣. Rejoice and be glad, O Virgin Mary, alleluia.

℟. *Because the Lord is truly risen, alleluia.*

Let us pray. O God, who by the Resurrection of Your Son, our Lord Jesus Christ, granted joy to the whole world: grant, we beg You, that through the intercession of the Virgin Mary, His Mother, we may lay hold of the joys of eternal life. Through the same Christ our Lord. ℟. *Amen.*

Self-Offering to Mary

HOLY Mary, Immaculate Virgin, Mother of God, I choose you for my Mother and advocate. Let me not depart from you today, but help me to do my duty for the sake of your divine Son. Let me be your devoted servant; assist me in all my actions, and forsake me not at the hour of my death. Amen.

Invocations

O Mary, conceived without sin, pray for us who have recourse to you.

———————

REMEMBER, O Virgin Mother of God, as you stand in the sight of the Lord, to speak for us, your little children.

———————

PRAY for us, O holy Mother of God, that we may be made worthy of the promises of Christ.

For Spiritual Protection

HOLY Virgin Mary, Mother of Jesus and my Mother, keep me free from sin and protect me in all dangers of soul and body. Help me today in my work; help me to be faithful to you so that I may give glory to God and save my soul. Amen.

For a Happy Death

JESUS, Mary, and Joseph, I give you my heart and my soul.

Jesus, Mary, and Joseph, assist me in my last agony.

Jesus, Mary, and Joseph, may I breathe forth my soul in peace at the end with you. Amen.

For the Holy Souls

JESUS, Mary, and Joseph, give eternal rest to the poor souls.

Jesus, Mary, and Joseph, let perpetual light shine upon them. May they rest in peace. Amen.

Mary the Morning Star

HOLY Mother Mary, I place myself under your loving protection and ask the help of your intercession.

Immaculate Mary, Morning Star, Star of the Sea, light the way for me.

May I be cheerful and pleasant to others this day and especially to those in my own home. Amen.

Mother of Sorrows

MOTHER of God, look down upon a poor sinner who has recourse to you. Dear Mother, I put my trust in you. You stood beneath the Cross and saw your Son die for us sinners because He wished so much to save us.

O good Mother, O Mother of Mercy, have pity on us, your small children. Amen.

The Litany of Loreto

LORD, have mercy.
Christ, have mercy.
Lord, have mercy.
Christ, hear us.
Christ, graciously hear us.
God, the Father of heaven, *have mercy on us.*
God the Son, Redeemer of the world,
have mercy on us.
God, the Holy Spirit,
have mercy on us.
Holy Trinity, one God,
have mercy on us.
Holy Mary, *pray for us.**
Holy Mother of God,
Holy Virgin of virgins,
Mother of Christ,
Mother of the Church,
Mother of Divine grace,
Mother most pure,
Mother most chaste,
Mother inviolate,
Mother undefiled,
Mother most amiable,
Mother most admirable,
Mother of good counsel,
Mother of our Creator,
Mother of our Savior,
Virgin most prudent,
Virgin most venerable,
Virgin most renowned,
Virgin most powerful,
Virgin most merciful,
Virgin most faithful,
Mirror of justice,
Seat of wisdom,
Cause of our joy,
Spiritual vessel,
Vessel of honor,
Singular vessel of devotion,
Mystical rose,
Tower of David,
Tower of ivory,
House of gold,
Ark of the covenant,
Gate of heaven,
Morning star,
Health of the sick,
Refuge of sinners
Comforter of the afflicted,
Help of Christians,
Queen of angels,
Queen of patriarchs,
Queen of prophets,
Queen of apostles,
Queen of martyrs,
Queen of confessors,
Queen of virgins,
Queen of all saints,
Queen conceived without original sin,
Queen assumed into heaven,
Queen of the most holy Rosary,
Queen of peace,
Lamb of God, You take away the sins of the world; *spare us O Lord!*

* *Pray for us is repeated after each invocation*

Lamb of God, You take away the sins of the world; *graciously hear us, O Lord!*

Lamb of God, You take away the sins of the world: *have mercy on us.*

℣. Pray for us. O holy Mother of God.

℞. *That we may be made worthy of the promises of Christ.*

Let us pray

G RANT, we beseech You, O Lord God, to Your servants that we may rejoice in continual health of mind and body; and by the glorious intercession of blessed Mary ever Virgin, we may be delivered from present trials and enjoy forever the happiness of heaven. We ask this through Christ our Lord. ℞. *Amen.*

The Litany of the Blessed Virgin Mary

The following litany is part of the newly approved *Order of Crowning an Image of the Blessed Virgin Mary,* The core of the litany lies in its explanation of Mary's Queenship.

Lord, have mercy.
Lord, have mercy.
Christ, have mercy.
Christ, have mercy.
Lord, have mercy.
Lord, have mercy.
God, our Father in heaven, *have mercy on us.*

God the Son, Redeemer of the world, *have mercy on us.*
God, the Holy Spirit, *have mercy on us.*
Holy Trinity, one God, *have mercy on us.*

Holy Mary, *pray for us.**
Holy Mother of God,
Most honored of virgins,
Chosen daughter of the Father,
Mother of Christ the King,
Glory of the Holy Spirit,
Virgin daughter of Zion,
Virgin poor and humble
Virgin gentle and obedient,
Handmaid of the Lord
Mother of the Lord,
Helper of the Redeemer,
Full of grace,
Fountain of beauty,
Model of virtue,
Finest fruit of the redemption,
Perfect disciple of Christ,
Untarnished image of the Church,
Woman transformed,
Woman clothed with the sun,
Woman crowned with stars,
Gentle Lady,
Gracious Lady,
Our Lady,
Joy of Israel,
Splendor of the Church,
Pride of the human race,
Advocate of grace,
Minister of holiness,
Champion of God's people,
Queen of love,
Queen of mercy,
Queen of peace,
Queen of angels,
Queen of patriarchs and prophets,
Queen of apostles and martyrs,
Queen of confessors and virgins,
Queen of all saints,
Queen conceived without original sin,
Queen assumed into heaven,
Queen of all the earth,
Queen of heaven,
Queen of the universe,
Lamb of God, You take away the sins of the world; *spare us, O Lord.*
Lamb of God, You take away the sins of the world; *hear us, O Lord.*
Lamb of God, You take away the sins of the world; *have mercy on us.*

* *Pray for us* is repeated after each invocation.

℣. Pray for us, O glorious Mother of the Lord.
℟. *That we may become worthy of the promises of Christ.*

Let Us Pray

GOD of mercy,
listen to the prayers of Your servants
who have honored Your handmaid Mary as
   Mother and Queen.
Grant that by Your grace
we may serve You and our neighbor on earth
and be welcomed into Your eternal kingdom.

We ask this through Christ our Lord.
℟. *Amen.*

The Name of Mary

MARY, my Mother, your precious name
floods my heart with love, your kindness is my inspiration and my hope; please kindle within me love's bright flame, enlighten my way, and give me the spiritual strength that I need now and always. Amen.

Prayer of St. Aloysius Gonzaga

MOST holy Mary, our Lady, to your faithful care and special keeping, and to the bosom of your mercy, today and every day, and particularly at the hour of my death, I commend myself, both soul and body.

All my hope and consolation, all my trials and miseries, my life and the end of my life, I commit to you, that, through your most holy intercession and by your merits, all my actions may be directed and ordered according to your will and that of your divine Son. Amen.

Prayer of St. Alphonsus Liguori

O Mother of God, Mary most holy, how many times I have sinned, but you, in your kind mercy, have rescued me.

Help me to overcome the hardness of my heart; gently draw me to place all my trust in you.

Loving Mother, preserve me from sin by your graces. O my Queen, I am grateful for all your many mercies and blessings.

I love you, next to God, above all things. Permit not that I ever turn my back on you. Through your intercession keep me close to your Son.

O Mary, I know that I will certainly condemn myself if I leave you. Do not let me ever forsake you. How could I forget the love you have for me?

No one surely is lost who has recourse to you. My Mother, do not leave me to rely solely on my own poor strength. I am so weak and childish. Grant that I will always come to you for help.

Save me, my hope, so that I may rejoice with you in heaven. Amen.

Act of Consecration to the Immaculate Heart of Mary

O Mary, Virgin most powerful and Mother of mercy, Queen of Heaven and refuge of sinners, we consecrate ourselves to you.

We offer you our lives, our hearts, and souls, our bodies, and all that we do.

We desire that you will be always in our homes, blessing our families and all of our loved ones. May your motherly love be with each one of us always.

We pledge ourselves to try to imitate your Son in our daily lives. Help us to courageously practice our faith in our pagan world and to strive ever in our lives to show the kindness of Jesus.

O glorious Mother of God and loving Mother of humans, we dedicate ourselves to your adorable Son; may His love fill our hearts and the hearts of all, so there will be peace in our homes and families, peace in our country, and peace in the world. Amen.

To Our Lady of Perpetual Help

BEHOLD, O Mother of Perpetual Help, one who is a poor sinner but who has recourse to you with all confidence. O Mother of Mercy, have pity on me. I call to you, Refuge of Sinners and my hope.

Help me for the love of Jesus. Hold out your hand to me. Praise God and give Him glory for me. And thank Him for His countless blessings.

My confidence in you is a sign of my eternal salvation, the saints have said. With your help, I will overcome my problems and difficulties and troubles.

I am fearful because I am weak; give me strength, dearest Mother. I run to you like a small child; you are my help and my courage, my light and my understanding. Mary most sweet, bless me always. Amen.

For the Sick and the Dying

O Mother of help, please assist the sick and the dying. Give your special love to those who die today. Help all the poor souls in purgatory.

Blessed Lady, do not delay to come to our aid. Assist those who are in need, in particular those who are hungry in soul and body.

What comfort you bring us. We are most grateful, dear Mother. What tenderness and kindness you have for your devoted children.

Amiable Mother, I call to you for myself and all who are troubled. You are the dispenser of many graces, rich in blessings. Come to us, your children, in our spiritual poverty. Assist us, please. Amen.

In Time of Worry

MANY times, dear Blessed Mother, I worry and am anxious. Please take these worries from me so that, at peace, I may help others, and think less of myself.

You are the advocate of the most miserable, the abandoned; you are the special friend of sinners. Help us. Come to our assistance. I commend myself to you and place in your hands all souls in need. Amen.

For Final Perseverance

I am your faithful servant, gentle Mother. Protect me and my loved ones and all who are in need this day. Give us final perseverance, to be faithful and true to your Son to the end, as you were. You are our model and example, Mother. Amen.

To Mary Our Mother

O dear Mother, we are your children, the children of your heart. Help us. We call to you our Mother, we who have the great joy of calling you Mother because Jesus on the Cross gave us to you, and we beg for your maternal care. Through your intercession, may we attain the happiness of eternal life. Amen.

Holy Mary, Help the Helpless

HOLY Mary, help the helpless, strengthen the fearful, comfort the sorrowful, pray for the people, plead for the clergy, intercede for all women consecrated to God; may all who keep your sacred commemoration experience the might of your assistance. Amen.

To Mary Immaculate

YOU are all fair, O Mary, and the original stain was never in you. You are the glory of Jerusalem, the joy of Israel, the honor of our people. You are the advocate of sinners, O Mary, Virgin most prudent, Mother most merciful; please pray for us. Intercede for us with our Lord Jesus, your Son. Amen.

A Prayer from the Ambrosian Liturgy

PETER who said he would die with Jesus ran way. Thomas who said, "Let us all die with Him," forsook Him, as did all the Apostles. Jesus was led forth alone to Calvary— and met His Immaculate Mother. Praise Jesus and His holy Mother. Amen.

Living Close to Jesus

O Mary, you lived so close to Jesus. Even when He was absent, He was in your heart. Pray for us, your children, that we may always live close to Christ. You were the servant of God, dear Mary. That is why you were joyful.

Help us to imitate you. Our troubles begin when in pride we try to run everything our way. Be our Mother indeed and protect us.

We are small children and we badly need your helping hand. Amen.

Prayer of Abbot Louis of Blois

O Mary, most sweet Virgin Mother of our Lord, most glorious Queen of Heaven, intercede for me with your Son.

Dear Mother, you are the merciful protector of the oppressed.

You are the support of the weak and infirm.

You are the refuge of the afflicted sinners.

Please look with your eyes of pity upon us.

By your intercession let my heart be inflamed with a greater love for your Son.

O all you glorious angels and blessed saints, intercede for me.

O my Guardian Angel, appointed by God as my sure companion and guardian, pray for me as I make my journey through this valley of tears.

O Mother Mary, intercede with Jesus on my behalf, so that one day I may be with your Son and with you and contemplate your beautiful faces in our heavenly home. Amen.

A Prayer of St. Anselm

I praise you, O holy Virgin Mary; give me strength against evil. Give me, please, the strength to humbly pray. Give me the strength to praise God with you, my Mother.

When Jesus was born it was the birth on earth of joy, hope, and comfort. The world was made light. Happy are we that you consented to His desire and made it possible for Him to enter His world. You, O Mary, brought Him forth, and we are most grateful.

You, dear Mother, sacrificed so much for us. Please, bless me a sinner and help me on my journey, so that, O Lady, just as at the Nativity, there will be joy.

Pray for me, Mother, pray to your sweet Son for me, for I am in need of your maternal prayers. Amen.

To Be Devoted to Mary

O holy Mary, our Lady, into your hands I give myself, body and soul. God chose you from among all creatures to be the Mother of Christ Jesus. I beseech you that I may ever be devoted to you, Blessed Mother, and by your intercession find mercy and favor with your Son, so that I may one day gain salvation and enter into our heavenly home. Amen.

A Prayer of St. Bernadette

O most holy Mother of Jesus, you felt the utter desolation of your Son dying on the cross. Please, help me in my hour of need. O Mother I come to you with anguish of heart; from your heart I seek courage and strength.

O most holy Mother of Jesus, assist me when I feel lonely and fearful.

And do you saints in paradise, who have passed through this life of trials, also have compassion on those who now must bear the burdens of life. Obtain for us the grace to be faithful unto death. Amen.

To Mary Our Hope

MOST holy Mary, my Lady, to your faithful care and special keeping, I dedicate myself. Keep me in your mercy day and night. And in particular be with me as you were with Joseph and Jesus at the hour of their death.

You are my hope, O Mary. In all my trials and troubles, be with me and I will be safe. Through your intercession and by your prayers I will always be protected, dear Mother. Amen.

To the Mother of Peace

WITH all my heart I honor you, dear Mother. Bless me and guard me, guide me and keep me.

You are my consolation and my comfort. Blessed are you.

Break down the walls of hatred and prejudice in the world and bring peace for all men.

Mother of God, we sing your praise. Inspire us to love your Son more. Amen.

Abandonment to Mary

VIRGIN full of goodness, I entrust my life to you. If you will not help me, where can I turn? But all the saints have said that you help all your children who go to you, even the worst sinner.

I pray for myself and for all sinners. I pray for the poor souls in purgatory.

May your beautiful motherly care always be with me. May I be humble as you were humble. Pride blocks the heart, and Jesus cannot come in. May you, O Mother, ever be my model in humility and resignation to the will of God. Amen.

Prayer to Mary

Composed by Pope John Paul II for the Marian Year

MOTHER of the Redeemer,
[in this year dedicated to you,]
with great joy we call you blessed.

In order to carry out His providential plan of
salvation,
God the Father chose you before the creation
of the world.
You believed in His love and obeyed His
word.

The Son of God desired you for His Mother
when He became Man to save the human
race.
You received Him with ready obedience and
undivided heart.

The Holy Spirit loved you as His mystical
spouse
and He filled you with singular gifts.
You allowed yourself to be led
by His hidden and powerful action.

On the eve of the third Christian Millennium,
we entrust to you the Church
which acknowledges you and invokes you as
Mother.
On earth you preceded the Church in the pil-
grimage of faith:
comfort her in her difficulties and trials,
and make her always the sign and instrument

of intimate union with God
and of the unity of the whole human race.

To you, Mother of Christians,
we entrust in a special way
the peoples who are celebrating
[during the Marian Year]
the sixth Centenary or the Millennium
of their acceptance of the Gospel.
Their long history is profoundly marked by
devotion to you.
Turn toward them your loving glance;
give strength to those who are suffering for
the faith.

To you, Mother of the human family and of
the nations,
we confidently entrust the whole of humanity,
with its hopes and fears.
Do not let it lack the light of true wisdom.
Guide its steps in the ways of peace.
Enable all to meet Christ,
the Way and the Truth and the Life.

Sustain us, O Virgin Mary, on our journey of
faith
and obtain for us the grace of eternal salvation.
O clement, O loving, O sweet Mother of God
and our Mother, Mary!

THE ROSARY

THE Rosary is Mary's special prayer. According to pious tradition, when St. Dominic was weary and discouraged from trying to preach to the heretics and getting nowhere, the Blessed Mother appeared to him and gave him the Rosary. It brought new courage, hope, and inspiration.

In reciting the Rosary one can think of the words of the Hail Mary and Our Father or reflect on the various mysteries. On Monday and Thursday, the Joyful Mysteries are recited; on Tuesday and Friday, the Sorrowful Mysteries; and on Wednesday, Saturday, and Sunday, the Glorious Mysteries. A mystery is announced with each Our Father (except the first).

The Joyful Mysteries. (1) The Annunciation: Mary is asked to be the Mother of the Messiah; (2) the Visitation: Mary journeys to help her elderly cousin Elizabeth who is going to have a child; (3) the Nativity: Christmas; (4) the Presentation: the Child is presented to God in the Temple; (5) Finding the Lost Child: Jesus at the age of twelve is lost in Jerusalem and found in the Temple.

The Sorrowful Mysteries. (1) The Agony in the Garden; (2) the Scourging by the Soldiers; (3) the Crowning with Thorns; (4) Jesus Is Made to Carry His Cross; (5) the Crucifixion.

The Glorious Mysteries. (1) Easter; (2) The Ascension: Jesus returns to Heaven; (3) Pentecost: the Holy Spirit comes to give courage and light to the Apostles; (4) the Assumption: Mary is reunited with her Son in heaven; (5) The Coronation: Mary is crowned Queen of Heaven.

There are other reflections that come to a person in reciting Mary's Rosary. The theme of the *Joyful Mysteries* is kindness. How kind Mary was at the Annunciation to say Yes to God so Jesus could be our Savior; how kind she was at the Visitation to go and help her elderly cousin; how kind Mary was at Christmas not to complain because things were so difficult; how kind she was at the Presentation not to plunge into self-pity when the prophet said a sword would pierce her heart; how kind was Mary in finding the Child Jesus in the temple not to complain loudly but to "keep all these things, pondering them in the heart."

The theme of the *Sorrowful Mysteries* is love. As we go through each of the sad and terrible events of Christ's suffering on Good Friday, we think of how much agony He endured for love of us.

The theme of the *Glorious Mysteries* is reunion. Reunions are always very happy times. At Easter Jesus was reunited to the

Apostles, after dying on the cross; they had given up all hope, and again He was with them. At the Ascension, the Son was reunited with the Father in heaven. At Pentecost, the Holy Spirit united His bravery and light to the fearful Apostles and made them courageous soldiers for Christ. At the Assumption Mary was reunited with Jesus in heaven—we can only begin to imagine the joy. At the Coronation, Mary, now Queen of Heaven, is in a place of honor where she in a special way is joined with her children on earth and can shower upon us countless blessings.